START THE COUNTDOWN

A PROPHETIC ALLEGORY FOR
RISING REGIONS OF REFUGE

MICHAEL FICKESS

Start the Countdown: A Prophetic Allegory for Rising Regions of Refuge
by Michael Fickess
Copyright 2016

First Edition.
Distributed by Ever-Increasing Glory Publications, LLC.
Visit www.michaelfickess.com for more information. Wholesale orders available through Amazon.com's expanded distribution network.

Unless otherwise indicated, all Scripture quotations are taken from the Holy Bible, New International Version (NIV), copyright 1978 by International Bible Society.

With the exception of short quotations of one page or less, no part of this book may be reproduced or transmitted in any form or by means electronic or mechanical, including photocopying, recording, or by an information storage and retrieval system, without written permission from the author.

All rights reserved.
Printed in the United States of America.

Cover Design: Michael Fickess
Internal Layout Design: Michael Carter

ISBN—978-1-53491-443-8; 1-53491-443-9

ENDORSEMENTS

"If your desire is to take a prophetic stroll *back to the future,* you will want to read "Start The Countdown" by Michael Fickess. In this book, Michael uses his extraordinary gift of blending prophetic revelation with science fiction. The result is a marriage of heavenly and earthly experiences, revealing biblical truths. As this story unravels, you will gain better understanding of the supernatural God we serve and how His angelic hosts interact with mankind.

I related to this book on a personal level because much of what Michael discusses are things my late husband Bob Jones taught, such as angels, portals, "houses of prayer, praise and prophecy," cities of refuge, the coming glory, and the greater works. Michael also sheds light on the maturity of the saints and their launching forward into the next move of God.

I would highly recommend "Start The Countdown" if you desire to learn more of the Father's truths and mysteries through an exciting prophetic journey with a sci-fi twist."

—**Bonnie Jones**
Bob and Bonnie Jones Ministries
www.bobjones.org

"Jesus brought Michael and I together a few years ago, when I was asked to teach on entering the heavenly realms at *Comenius School for Creative Leadership*. I noticed that the hearts of the students there were more intensely excited on waiting on the Lord than in other places that I had been. I asked God, "why is it like this here?" With questions like that there is usually more than one answer. To my surprise, Michael was deeply involved with many of the answers. He was teaching small groups in an open format to interact with the Kingdom of Heaven.

There was radical intervention in the destinies of these youth. His heart was in agreement with the Holy Spirit in teaching, directing, and equipping the next generation not only for entering the heavenlies, but also understanding, interacting with, and bringing the heavenlies on earth. There is no doubt in my mind that those who have been with Michael for any length of time have encountered Jesus.

With this in mind, prepare yourself, for inside these pages resides great insight into the potential dichotomy of humanity. This book provides a heavenly perspective on the upcoming times and generations. He has done an amazing job in describing this open spiritual experience with such vibrancy that you cannot help but to go there with him. May the Holy Spirit use this book to encourage, equip and advance you."

—Lyn Kost
Prophetic Teacher, Worship Leader, and Administrator for Bob and Bonnie Jones Ministries | www.bobjones.org

Table of Contents

INTRODUCTION
7

IN THE GARDEN
15

SURVEYING THE FALL
23

COUNSEL AND POWER
34

MISSION CONTROL
46

CATCHING UP WITH THE FUTURE
53

GOING UP
63

INTO ZION
70

THE ROAD HOME
77

SETTING THE TABLE
87

THE LAUNCH PAD
95

AFTERWORD
103

Introduction

"Every science fiction movie I have ever seen, any one that's worth its weight in celluloid, warns us about things that ultimately come true."
—**Steven Spielberg**

This book embodies two things I love—*prophetic revelation* and *science fiction*. This may seem like a strange combination, but there are striking similarities between these two genres. Prophetic writers and science fiction writers are both concerned with illuminating aspects of the *present* that the general population tends to ignore. Their art is one of discerning trends and seeing new possibilities.

Start the Countdown

Some of the most valuable insights and accurate predictions over the last century have come from science fiction writers, sci-fi movies, and comic books. This is because science fiction writers are fearless. They march into the dark arena of the apocalypse without hesitation—worlds are destroyed and explored, civilizations rise to towering heights and collapse again, and heroes rise out of the desolation, dreaming impossible dreams. Renewed interest in comic books and science fiction movies is rooted in the deeper awareness that our lives are half-lived, our spiritual potential unexplored and unrealized. For most Americans, a visit to the theater is simply a chance to be entertained. However, I have written this book for those who long to *be* the next Luke Skywalker because they see the full weight of what it means to be a "new creation" (2 Corinthians 5:17).

In the 21st century, we tend to consign the Creator of the cosmos to Sunday morning services and sporadic moments of devotion. However, I hope this book will point the reader back to the exciting reality of Christ's eternal supremacy over the entire cosmos.

Introduction

Seeing our desperate struggle under the curse of the Fall of man, Christ shed His blood to purchase a glorious restoration that will far outweigh anything that came before. Then, after purchasing "all authority" to restore the cosmos and upgrade it with much greater glory, He handed the keys to *us*. Now, the only way for us to use these keys properly is to truly become the "new creation" we are called to be.

When properly understood, the scriptures contain far more drama and possibility than the greatest story any science fiction story writer could conjure. This book is intended to explore the most potent promises of the Bible, which we will need to understand more deeply in order to navigate the challenges of our times.

PROPHETIC INSIGHT AND CREATIVITY

I associate this prophetic allegory with science fiction because this book includes many elements of science fiction, such as time travel, space travel, and the kind of apocalyptic destruction and renewal we see in popular sci-fi movies. However, this book is different than science fiction because it examines our immense challenges and unrealized potential from a uniquely *prophetic* perspective. This book chronicles some of my most riveting encounters with God. However, despite the gravity of the subject matter in some of these chapters, this book was fun to write because I used my creative liberty to create new characters and plot events to embellish the story. I took this liberty because I believe that revelation from the Father may come in profound trances and visions or on the blank canvas of the redeemed imagination, as He illumines our thoughts by His Spirit.

The fast pace of the plot is intended to be as thrilling and terrifying as your favorite post-apocalyptic sci-fi movie. I hope this unique style will turn the reader's imagination back to the profound truth of Christ's accomplishments.

It is difficult to chronicle the process of writing a book like this because prophetic confirmations came to me in so many different ways. For example, in July of 2013 I had an open vision of red dust storms sweeping across America. I was terrified and unsure

Introduction

of what to make of this. I wrote down what I saw and set it aside. A few days later, I heard a recording of John Paul Jackson prophesying about dust storms in America that would be measured in *inches*. A few years later, the movie *Interstellar* came out, illustrating this warning in a way the whole nation could comprehend. Many of the core revelations of this book came in a similar manner—revelation was followed by *confirmation* from different sources. Instead of detailing each of these occurrences, I present these insights in simple narrative form because I trust my readers' discernment.

This book is in the same *genre* as my other prophetic allegory, *The Restoration of All Things*. However, my previous book highlighted the restoration of the *heart of man*, while this book explores the immense environmental challenges we face and how to deal with them. The scriptures are our plumb line for assessing revelation. However, our interpretation of scripture is often misguided by religious traditions that stand in opposition to what the Spirit of Truth wants to reveal. Hopefully, the insights in this book will allow you to see the most relevant truths of the

Bible with a fresh perspective.

For those who share the same love for science fiction that I do, I have incorporated a fun and subtle feature in this book. There are allusions to classic science fiction stories and movies interspersed throughout the book, hidden like "Easter eggs" for the reader to find.

This is something I have actually done in every book I have written. Each book contains hidden connections and subtle references that are like a trail for discerning readers to follow. For example, the orange cloud appearing on the front of *Enoch's Blessing,* my first book, is a symbol that is later explained fully in chapter ten of the sequel, *Paths of Ever-Increasing Glory.* The habit of hiding "Easter eggs" in my written works is something I adopted from movie directors like J.J. Abrams and Steven Spielberg, who often use this technique to honor films that inspired them or to hint at their next project. I treat every project the Lord gives me very seriously. However, if we are not having fun along the way, then we are missing something critical.

Introduction

Although this is primarily a prophetic chronicle, the footnotes in this book are designed to lead the reader back to searching the scriptures. I recommend a first reading to encounter the story's central message and a second reading to explore the hundreds of scripture references supporting it. This way, the Biblical concepts expressed in this book can be revisited and fully searched out by hungry hearts.

We must begin to infuse all of our teaching with even more Biblical truth because multitudes are about to be swept into the kingdom of God in the next great move of God. These new believers will be hungry for greater understanding and careful training on every matter, and I want this book to be a quality resource for them.

According to the scriptures, the primary purpose of prophecy under the New Covenant is to **"encourage, comfort, and strengthen"** believers (see 1 Corinthians 14:3). In times of peace and prosperity, we do not value our spiritual gifts as much as we should. However, we are about to face an hour when we will desperately need the kind of encouragement, comfort, and strength that only the eternal Spirit of God can impart to us. I hope the message of this book will inspire the reader to press in for these greater gifts now, so we may all be better equipped to face the challenges of tomorrow.

chapter 10

IN THE GARDEN

It was something my grandmother taught me to do years ago. *"Speak to your garden. Talk to the plants. Show them love. You'll always see a difference."* I looked around and wondered what she would say if she were here with me now.

The morning sun streamed into the small plot, shining through translucent green leaves and turning the dew drops into little diamonds. Hollyhocks, phlox, and roses woke up from their slumber to show off their colors. Salad greens and root crops burst from the soil, promising that it would be a very good year. The trellised tomatoes seemed to have grown at least two more inches. The fresh nitrogen from last night's booming thunderstorm must have helped. The chickens eagerly picked through the kitchen scraps I gave them, while one sang its laying song in the nesting box.

As I walked along the well-trod paths, I noted every little curiosity. Orb webs hung heavy with the moisture of the storm. Squirrels made a mess of the bird feeders again. Young rabbits darted into the brush at the back of the lot. A faint fragrance of rosemary and mint wafted up from the path, as my feet brushed against the perennial herbs beginning to spread near the path.

This was that special time of year in the Carolinas when everything that is planted begins to show its blossoms and set its fruit. Blights and diseases did not have time to take root yet. The pests had barely awakened from their winter sabbatical.

A breeze began to blow on the garden, and I closed my eyes. It was hard to believe life could have this much pleasure in it.

Suddenly, I felt the presence of the Lord

fill the garden. I became keenly aware that *He is right here, right now.* I took a deep breath and closed my eyes, wondering if the Spirit of the Lord wanted to tell me something. I kept my eyes closed for a long time, feeling the tangible weight of His peace upon me and listening as the breeze ruffled the leaves.

When I opened my eyes, the garden looked completely different. In addition to the beauty I saw before, I could see the pure white light of the Father streaming up through every tree, through every blade of grass. I could see His light shining in all of creation.

The light was not simply residing in each living thing, it was *moving through it,* regenerating, multiplying, growing, and beautifying. This light was much more beautiful than the flowers I was just admiring. It was more captivating than any of the curiosities that caught my attention only a few minutes before. This streaming light was unlike any light I had seen before, for it felt infused with a sense of love and well-being.

"This is a very dim shadow of what the

Father has prepared for you." I turned to see a portly middle-aged man dressed in clothes that looked like they were straight from the 1930's.

"Who are you?" I asked.

"I was a friend to Harry Ritter, your great-grandfather, and now I have been sent to you."

"Are you from the cloud of witnesses?" I asked with excitement.[1] The angel smiled and chuckled under his breath.

"No, but I did help Harry through all his years of farming. The righteous are never alone in any wholesome thing they pursue, but that doesn't mean they always *see* who is helping them.[2] It was my job to give Harry new ideas for managing his crops and tending his pastures so he could prosper. The Father loved him and wanted to bless him, as He does *all* His children. Most of His children don't recognize the true nature of the help they're getting, but they receive it nonetheless."

---
1   See Hebrews 12:1-3.
2   See Hebrews 1:14, Hebrews 13:2.

In the Garden

Changing the subject, the angel pointed to the garden and repeated his first words, "This is a very dim shadow of what the Father has prepared for you."[3]

Now that I had turned my attention to the angel, I could no longer see the light moving through the plants. However, I remembered how much light I saw in this small plot only a few minutes before.

"Once you've glimpsed the *first* garden, you can see its lingering light in all of creation, but the light of restoration that is coming is much greater. Your job is not to recreate Eden, but to join with others to bring a restoration that will be much greater than Eden."

The angel plucked a leaf from the base of the tomato plant I thought was very healthy. Pointing to a few small brown spots, he said, "Can you see the early blight setting in here? The curse of the Fall has caused the glorious light the Father invested in His creation to gradually fade. Every plague, blight, and defect in creation is a result of the fading of this light...even your own DNA is affected

---

[3] See 1 Corinthians 2:9.

by this. The challenge you face is, you are entering into the days of Noah again—a time when these kinds of plagues and curses will increase, because the fading of the light is accelerated by wickedness and godlessness."

"You are comfortable in your own garden because you have made it a refuge through prayer, declaration, and careful stewardship. However, even this refuge will not last long if you do not prepare for the storm that is coming."

I looked around as the angel spoke, surveying my hard work in the fruitful garden. I had invested *years* in it, and it was heartbreaking to consider losing it.

"The true root of all restoration is *love*. It is true that the Body of Christ will shine with greater love at the time when **"the love of most will grow cold"** (Matthew 24:12). It has already been preached that this love will bring in a great harvest of souls, even as wickedness increases in the world. However, most have not seen how the cruelty in the heart of man will impact *creation*. Just as the enemy seeks to destroy mankind, he is also seeking to destroy the whole creation. The same wickedness and cruelty that leads to suffering in mankind will also be directed at creation itself. This is a violence born of self-centeredness, hatred, and godlessness. Come now, there is much more I have to show you."

As he said these last words, we began to ascend high up into the atmosphere, the earth whirling around beneath us as we departed. In a matter of seconds, sunlight gave way to twilight and billowy clouds to smog, for we were now arriving at our new destination.

22

Chapter 9

SURVEYING THE FALL

When we stopped moving, we were suspended in the atmosphere high above China, looking down at the nation. Many of the rivers were stained toxic colors, with little but algae alive in them. In the cities, young families wore dust masks to shield themselves from the poison in the atmosphere. Millions of acres, once fertile fields, were now deserts where the soil itself was poison. Farming villages were filled with people dying of sicknesses from the toxins in the air, water, and soil.

"Is this the devastation that is coming?" I asked the angel.

"No, this is the devastation that already *is*. However, a destruction much greater than this will be coming to every nation if something is not done soon. This devastation does not stop at the arbitrary line that mankind draws on a map."

When he said this, we moved even higher up in the atmosphere, and I began to see the curvature of the earth. I thought about the ocean currents and the jet streams, constantly moving around the world, re-circulating the atmosphere and the water. I glimpsed a dust storm that would sweep from nation to nation. Then, I saw a thirst for clean, drinkable water—a desperate thirst strong enough to trigger wars.

"The enemy's plan is to destroy creation *itself*, out of hatred for the Father and His children. However, he can only do this by perverting man's sovereignty—by replacing wise and holy stewardship with *greed, lust, and wickedness*. But it does not have to be this way."

Surveying the scene before me, I realized that the poisoning of our own water, air, and soil was an ultimate expression of evil. I saw

Surveying the Fall

how man's wickedness brought desolation to the earth and how this desolation made man even more wicked. My thoughts wandered into the future, and I saw the earth heave and tremble with great earthquakes, as the earth's mantle travailed under the weight of rising wickedness.

The angel waited for me to finish this glimpse and then broke in, "The land cries out. The earth is gripped with longing for restoration, but it is a restoration that only the children of God can impart."[1]

Attempting to find a way out of this line of thinking, I protested, "But what about all the laws we have passed to reduce pollution and fix these problems? What about all the people who really care about the Father's creation? What about the new technologies being developed? Hasn't the Father already begun to give us the answers to fix these problems?"

The angel smiled again. "The Father's loving-kindness is everlasting. He has used many of these things to hold back winds of adversity for many decades for the sake of

---

1 See Romans 8:18-25.

the righteous.[2] In fact, many new ideas and technologies given to unsaved entrepreneurs came *because* of the prayers of the saints. However, don't be fooled. The storm that is coming is much larger than most have anticipated. This storm will be so catastrophic that many will despair of life, and others will even attempt to leave the planet."

Filled with hopelessness, I asked quietly, "Why would the Father allow this storm? Why not hold it back for a few more generations?"

With a twinkle in his eye, the angel replied, "Have you not seen yet? This storm will not accomplish what the enemy thinks it will. The enemy's time is very short.[3] In his short-sighted fury, he will attempt to stir up the hatred of mankind until great suffering floods the whole world. However, he has not been allowed to see the Father's blueprints for these times. The Father has specifically designed this storm for the training and raising up of His Holy Ones. For this is also the hour when the great City of God is being built. This is the time when He will establish Zion on the earth, where nation is reconciled with nation

---

2 See Revelation 7:1-3.
3 See Revelation 12:12.

until creation is restored.[4] It is a time when His people will learn to rule and reign with love and power, creating vast regions of refuge wherever they abide. Try as he might, the enemy cannot stop the kingdom of heaven from displacing every other kingdom in these times."[5]

The angel pointed up to the sky. A small rock was approaching at a fierce velocity. As soon as I saw it, I moved closer in the Spirit and examined it. It was made of a material I had never encountered before. At first glance, it seemed to be black, but as I looked deeper into it, I thought I saw many different colors. It seemed to phase in and out of different spectrums as I tried to determine what it was made of. Whatever it was, it was very weighty and charged with limitless energy.

"What is it?" I asked the angel.

"The revelation of the kingdom of heaven that is about to come will completely change how people think and interact with creation. This small stone is just one particular revelation about the creative light of the

---

[4] See Isaiah 2:2-5, Isaiah 11:6-9.
[5] See Daniel 2:44, Revelation 11:15-17.

Father.[6] Many are about to learn that the same God who said 'Let there be light' in the beginning now abides in them. They are about to discover the authority they have in Christ, Who reigns supreme over all creation. The reason it appears black to you is because you have no frame of reference for this kind of light. Your mind interprets anything you cannot understand as darkness.

In time, you will learn to see a higher spectrum of light, the same spectrum that emanates from the Lamb Who is seated on the throne.[7] This is what you saw briefly in the garden. However, these kinds of deeper truths can only be understood fully by looking at them *through* the Lamb. He is always the center of what the Father is doing. Looking into anything *apart* from Him is dangerous because He is the fountainhead of everything the Spirit reveals."

I thought about Daniel chapter two, where the prophet described a small stone that will demolish all the kingdoms of this world. "Is this the stone that Daniel prophesied?" I asked.

---

[6] See the "Creative Light" teaching by Ian Clayton, available on Company of Burning Hearts Podcast.
[7] See Revelation 4:2-3.

Surveying the Fall

"Not at all. That stone is so glorious that I'm not sure you would be able to perceive more than a fraction of the light it carries. This smaller stone is only one of many revelations the Father is giving to raise up His Holy Ones in this time."

As soon as the angel said, "This is only one of many...", I saw an endless array of shining lights, each one headed for the earth like a blazing comet on a mission. Each of these represented a different revelation the Father was imparting to His children to prepare them for what was coming.[8]

They were marked with different phrases, like "new levels of worship," "sonship and reigning," and "consecrated priesthood." Each of these impacted the planet in a different place and then spread out from there to touch the whole globe.[9] As I saw them impact the earth, great glory would emanate from the impact site in cosmic shock waves.

"The enemy is bound to the earth, so he will do all he can to destroy it. However, the Father is now releasing a limitless assault of

---
8 See Joel 2:28-32.
9 See Habakkuk 2:14.

holy revelation and ancient mysteries that will constantly confound the enemy's plans.[10] He has no power to stop this heavenly artillery, which is why the saints will completely triumph in the end."[11]

Watching these revelations impact the earth was like watching a million stars collide all at once. Profusions of glory and power burst from each impact. I was reminded of what the Lord said about the end times—"**the stars will fall from the sky, and the heavenly bodies will be shaken**" (Matthew 24:29) I had always interpreted this to signify natural meteors or comets, not a series of divine revelations.

The angel pointed deeper into the cosmos, and I saw new stars being born in distant nebulae, their positions fixed forever as brilliant shining lights.

"It is true that the heavens and the earth are being shaken and that many new revelations are coming to earth. However, the Father's greatest prize is those who learn to become the new creation He has called them to be. As He raises up His holy ones, they will learn to shine

---

10 See Isaiah 45:3, 1 Corinthians 2:6-8.
11 See Revelation 19.

with a rising glory and gravity that outweighs any previous generation.[12]

They will carry great authority as lesser brothers of Christ, Who alone achieved supremacy over creation through His shed blood.[13] They will learn to administrate this redemption forever, reflecting the Father's glory and pleasure in His only Son."[14]

I was dismayed by what the angel said. "Isn't it dangerous for men to take on this much glory? I thought the Father would not "share His glory" with any man?[15] How can anyone have this much power and authority without being tempted to succumb to pride and fall, as Satan did in the beginning?"[16]

"The revelations the Father is releasing now will prevent this from happening. Those who rise to this level of power and authority will first be given revelations of the beauty and love of God that will completely change their core nature.[17] The Father will only grant power and

---

12 See Daniel 12:3.
13 See Romans 8:29, Colossians 1:15-20.
14 See Matthew 17:5, Romans 8:15, Galatians 4:6.
15 See Isaiah 42:8.
16 See Ezekiel 28:11-19.
17 See Eph. 3:16-19, 1 Cor. 13, 1 John 3:16-21.

authority in accordance with the level of *love* that each one is walking in. They will discover Zion and realize that much of their power and authority is rooted in holy community.

The reason you cannot imagine the level of power that some will walk in is because you have not yet plunged the depths of love in store *for yourself.* The great floods of worship, devotion, and consecration that are coming will raise up a holy priesthood that can properly handle this level of power because their hearts will be continually captivated by His love.[18] They will be simmering in His surpassing glory all the time."[19]

---

[18] See Ezekiel 47 for a prophetic depiction of rising spiritual water levels.
[19] See Luke 3:16, 2 Corinthians 3:10-18.

chapter 8

COUNSEL AND POWER

Our next stop on this spiritual journey was at the United Nations in New York City. It felt good to have my feet firmly planted on the earth again. We entered the front door unseen, walked past the security cameras undetected, and sat down in the last row of the General Assembly Hall.

As we sat down, the clock on the wall began to accelerate. As the clock hands spun, the people ran in and out, the lights flashed on and off and weeks, months, and years flashed before us. In the midst of this time, there were two sets of resolutions being passed.

The first set of resolutions was earnestly intended to fix serious problems in the natural environment before they happened. Although some nations saw this as a plot to control and manipulate the masses, many leaders were sincerely trying to save the planet. Although many were crying out "conspiracy," these resolutions were based on genuine concern, even if severely misguided.

There was a shift between these two sets of resolutions. There was a point at which the birth pangs in creation increased in frequency.[1] The earth groaned loud enough for everyone to hear it.[2] Ocean waves carried millions of dead sea creatures onto beaches until the stench filled the coasts. Earthquakes shook the world and volcanoes erupted. The weather became much more extreme and violent than anyone could have anticipated. Great dust storms swept across plains from nation to nation, while in other places, floods swept away whole towns and buried cities. This is when the famines began, even in first-world nations.

---

1 See Matthew 24:8.
2 See Romans 8:22.

Start the Countdown

When the second set of resolutions began, it became clear that governments were powerless to stop the terrifying scene unfolding. Instead of a desperation to hold on to control, there was a desperation to simply *survive* or save as many lives as possible. Governments began to crumble, one after another, as they proved their inability to deal with the reality of the trembling earth. I wondered if this was the time when the antichrist that was prophesied would arise, the time when a new global government would take center stage with deceptive "answers." Just as I began to follow this line of thinking, the angel placed his hand on my shoulder.

"I have not been sent to show you those things. Some things have been hidden by the Father until the proper time for them to be revealed. He wanted to show you how the kingdoms of this world will crumble in the time of the end. However, there will also be much more hope in this time than ever before.[3] Now, it is time to see the *other* side of the coin—the kingdom that cannot be shaken.[4] For it is *this* kingdom that will increase and fill

---
3   See Isaiah 60:1-3.
4   See Hebrews 12:28.

the earth in these times."

In a flash of light, we now found ourselves in a small traditional church in rural Pennsylvania. Even when full to capacity, this little church, hidden and nestled on a hilltop, could not have held more than about forty people. Similar to our visit to the United Nations, we entered the meeting unnoticed and the clock on the back wall began to spin through weeks, months, and years.

I became very alarmed as the number of people attending this church began to dwindle. The angel turned to me, smiling, and said, "Just keep watching." Eventually, there were only three people left.

The clock returned to its normal pace and I could hear them praying. Unseen to them, thousands of mighty angels—heralds, fiery seraphim, and glorious cherubim gathered around them, waiting for their next instructions.[5]

They spent a considerable amount of time just waiting on the Lord, asking for a

5   See Hebrews 1:7.

revelation of His will and looking deeper into His promises. Then, having received clear prophetic instructions, they prayed with confidence and authority.

A middle-aged African-American woman spoke out gently, "We rebuke this line of severe storms in Jesus' name. Father, stretch your canopy of protection over this region." Her voice was majestic and soothing and her words were measured like lines of poetry. As soon as she said this, several angels, who had the appearance of the wind, darted off to completely disrupt the destructive storms about to strike the region.

A young man began praying, "Father, we lift up the West Coast today. Spare the people and let them know that it was *Your mercy* that saved them." As soon as he prayed this, a legion of angels, who looked like glowing fire, left in swift flight to hold back the pillars of the earth. A large earthquake that was on God's calendar for a long time was broken up into several smaller ones that served as stern warnings, but carried much less destruction.

Then, a teenage girl began to pray with

childish simplicity, "Father, bring the birds back. Bring the flowers back. Bring the worshippers and God-lovers back until a tent of protection is stretched out all over this land. Let Your light flood in until the tide of darkness on the earth recedes."

As she prayed, the most powerful angels were released. These angels had great wooden stakes in their hands, and they marked out a region of refuge where the Lamb will spread His tent in a time of shaking.[6] The enemy was not allowed to touch this region because the land itself was blessed. Crops grew here and songbirds returned, even when they vanished elsewhere.[7] As people were ransacking and looting in other places, neighbors here still worked together to solve problems, freely borrowing, lending, and helping the needy, with no regard for themselves.

I looked over at the angel, who was standing next to the hard wooden pew I was sitting on. "It looks to me like this small prayer group of three people accomplished more than the United Nations in both sets

6   See Isaiah 54, Revelation 7:14-17.
7   See the stark contrast between the blessing and cursing of land in Deuteronomy 28.

of their resolutions.[8] However, when is this little group going to grow? Aren't there supposed to be great multitudes brought into the kingdom at this time?"[9]

The angel seemed alarmed at my dullness. "Don't you know that different churches and ministries have different callings? There is another church in this town that is discipling five thousand people right now, which is nearly the population of the entire town. They were training for this for decades. However, *this* fellowship was called to be a group of prophetic intercessors. Neither of these fellowships could survive these times without the other."[10]

"The territorialism that you currently see in the Body of Christ no longer exists in these times. Each fellowship knows its purpose and has a clear mission. In the past, the big church down the road tried to destroy this little fellowship because they saw it as a threat. This is why you saw its numbers shrink. Likewise, this little group used to pray

---

8   See Matthew 18:19-20.
9   See Revelation 7:9.
10 See 1 Corinthians 12:4-6.

against the big church and bind what they saw as its "spirit of conformity."[11] However, the Spirit of the Lord released a spirit of burning over this region in the last few decades that allowed each of these groups to move past these carnal distractions and truly love each other."[12]

I wondered, and hoped, that this would not be the only region of refuge in these times. I thought about the different regions I had visited and prayed for over the years.

The angel interrupted my thoughts again, "There are many different regions of refuge being raised up in these times. In the places where desperate governments will crumble and fall in the worst manner, it will leave a low place for the kingdom of heaven to flood in and take possession. Even though Christ has not yet come to restore all things, some of these regions will begin to access the powers of the age to come. Some regions will even be untouchable to the antichrist. These are the regions where people will be able to *choose* between hiddenness and the honor of

---

[11] See Galatians 5:14-15.
[12] See Isaiah 4:3-6, Galatians 5:16-26.

martyrdom."

As he began speaking about martyrdom, the earth began to tremble under our feet. "Is this another birth pang?" I asked.

"It is not what you think. The fellowship down the street is opening the gates of heaven with worship.[13] It is true that creation travails under the weight of wickedness and godlessness. This is when its trembling expresses pain and suffering. However, this is a different kind of trembling, for the land itself is drinking in the light, life, and love that flow from the Lamb. This entire region is being redeemed because the people here have learned to use worship and intercession to open heaven's gates and release a new flood of glory into the land."

The angel's words offended me because they were at odds with my own eschatology. "How can so much glory be released at a time when the whole world is being devastated with drought, war, and shaking?"

"The Lord compared these times to the

---
13 See Psalm 24:7-10, Psalm 87, Psalm 100:4.

days of Noah because all creation is groaning under the weight of man's wickedness. However, this does not mean that things will unfold in the exact same way," the angel answered.

He continued, "The first time the earth was destroyed, it was through a baptism of water. The flood in Noah's time swept away every trace of wickedness and godlessness from the earth. However, wickedness rose again in the heart of mankind, for the heart of man was the last vestige of darkness.

"This time, the earth is being baptized with Spirit and fire. The Spirit is being poured out on all flesh to restore the heart of mankind so that creation itself will be restored. A spirit of burning holiness is now purifying multitudes, carrying them from wickedness and godlessness to great consecration. This is the same multitude that John describes—they will be a countless number **"from every tribe, tongue, and nation"** who abides continually under the shadow of the Lamb (Revelation 7:9,15). **"He will lead them to springs of water and green pasture,"** even as the earth itself is scorched with judgment, wars, and environmental devastation (Revelation 7:17).

"The best way to prepare for these times is to learn to make the Lord your Shepherd now.[14] Those who lead peaceful, quiet, and godly lives in the decades leading up to this time will shine like the sun when midnight falls upon the world."[15]

As the angel gave these last few exhortations, a weighty peace began to increase within the room and upon me, until it was too much for me to take in. I fell on my face and went into a deep slumber, just as the angel finished his words.

---

14 See John 10:7-30, Psalm 23.
15 See 1 Timothy 2:1-4.

chapter 7

Mission Control

I dreamed I was at NASA's mission control center, watching the first manned flight to Mars. Technicians with headsets gazed on the massive plasma screens before them, watching the first footsteps on the red soil. This was soon followed by a series of pods which were quickly inflated for living and working spaces. I was surprised that there was not more excitement in the room. Instead of the kind of victorious celebration that accompanied the moon landing, there was a sense of desperation.[1] Sweat was beading up on the brows of the technicians, as they obsessed over what could go wrong.

1   Revelation 9:6.

"The situation on the ground is different now." I turned to see a great archangel, his high rank identified by the intricacy of his robes, his stature, and the great glory radiating from his face.

"When Apollo 11 landed, there was a joyous declaration of 'The Eagle has landed!' The astronauts landed their craft in the 'Sea of Tranquility' which signifies the peace that accompanied the nation in earlier times of exploration. However, that tranquility has now evaporated and they are now more like refugees desperately searching for a place of peace and safety.[2] This mission is not about demonstrating a nation's greatness. It is not about reaching higher and discovering more. This mission is about *survival*."

I remembered the vast dust storms I saw moving from nation to nation, the poisoning of the air, water, and soil, the terrifying trembling of the earth.[3] It was ironic that now mankind was exploring a place where dust storms were inevitable, the water was inaccessible, and the air was unbreathable.

---

2 See 1 Thessalonians 5:3.
3 See Revelation 8:6-13.

As I looked around the room, I noticed the technicians were not just monitoring the rocket launches and landings. Their eyes were fixed on screens which showed that creation itself was rapidly degrading. One screen showed highly abnormal solar activity—cycles of massive flares and coronal mass ejections, followed by cycles of sunspots that dwarfed any seen before.[4] Another monitor showed the magnetic core of the earth shifting in response, with the end result of weather patterns changing around the globe. The seasons were changing around the globe and crop failure was becoming the new norm.

Numb with disbelief, I looked back at the archangel. To my surprise, he was smiling and simply pointing up. It was clear he knew something I didn't.

"When the kingdoms of this world crumble, it means that the kingdom of God is already advancing at an unstoppable pace. The City of God is approaching, and its brilliant radiance is already beginning to overshadow this part of the cosmos.[5] This is why every indication is showing that things

---

[4] See Revelation 16:8, Revelation 19:17.
[5] See Revelation 21:2.

are about to end. In many ways, this is true. However, what is really ending? It is the end of night. It is the end of the curse. It is the end of sickness, degradation, and chaos. It is the end of the reign of demonic principalities and powers, and the end of human wickedness and cruelty.

However, this is also the beginning of the glorious dawn. Christ's millennial reign is so glorious that its radiance is spilling back through the fabric of space-time to overshadow this dark hour. Now, it is time for you to see *the Father's* "mission control" and discover what is on *His* mind."

As he said the last words, I was lifted up high into the heavens.[6] I saw a vast horizon that appeared like a thin gold line. Unlike the horizon of the earth with its gentle curvature, this horizon was a perfect line extending forever to the right and left. There were smaller trails leading to it and from it, like a network of golden paths.[7] Its golden radiance and beauty were beyond description. It was like a slice carved out of the space-time continuum, through which one could glimpse

---
6 See Ezekiel 8:3.
7 See Revelation 21:21.

the glorious eternal realms where the Father abides in perfect light and joy all the time.[8] I began to feel the intimate friendship of God—His beckoning to come abide *with* Him and walk with Him on golden paths that traverse high above the realm of time and space.[9]

As I looked into this golden dawn and the paths of gold that led to it, I felt ecstasy and power beyond anything I had felt before. I was reminded of the **"Highway of Holiness"** that Isaiah described, a path of transcendent power reserved for those who walk with God.[10] I remembered the veil that was torn when Christ said, **"It is finished!"**[11] I remembered when the Father beckoned John, **"Come up here, and I will show you what must take place after this..."**[12]

I lingered there a long time. The shadows around me vanished, and I was immersed in the radiant golden light. I could feel the smile of the Father upon me, for that light carried wave after wave of His *pleasure* and *desire* for

---

8 See Psalm 16:11.
9 See John 17:20-26, Ephesians 2:18.
10 See Isaiah 35:8.
11 See Matthew 27:51, John 19:30.
12 See Revelation 4:1.

me. This light also carried a transcendent power that I had never encountered before. I could comprehend things more clearly and quickly than ever before, for the golden light of the Father was beginning to penetrate my heart and mind. His light was working in my core nature, shaping my desires and longings to align with *His*.[13]

I began to hear sounds and see things I had no frame of reference for—deep groaning emanating from beyond the outer reaches of the universe. I realized this was the sound of the entire cosmos longing to be restored, but also the sound of the first waves of restoration unfolding.

It was not only I who needed the Father's intimate friendship. It was not only I whom He desired. His desire was invested in *the entire cosmos*, and I knew He intended to restore it fully.[14]

---

13   See Ps. 44:3, Ps. 89:15, Isaiah 2:5, 1 Jn 1:5-7.
14   See Revelation 21:1-5.

Chapter 6

CATCHING UP WITH THE FUTURE

"Should we wake him up?" the young girl asked with an excited whisper.

"He has been out for hours. I think it is time," answered the young man.[1]

"Honey, it's time. We have a lotta ground to cover today." The middle-aged African American woman shook my shoulder and roused me from the hard wooden pew. I was still at the small church in rural Pennsylvania. Standing to stretch my weary back, I could hear the songbirds announcing it was morning, as the first rays of golden light shone through the windows.

---

1 See Job 33:14-18, Daniel 8:18, Daniel 10:9.

Start the Countdown

The three prayer warriors waited for me to stretch and come to my senses before they introduced themselves as Lucy, Derek, and Martha.

"How am I still here?" I asked with surprise. "I thought I was just having a *spiritual* experience."

"*Still* here?" Martha laughed. "This is the first we've seen of you. If you need a shower or a fresh change of clothing, there's plenty of that at Zion Fellowship down the road. You look like you've been through the mill."

Lucy broke in to ease the awkwardness, "We were just about to start our prayer meeting. You're welcome to join us."

Derek made a gesture for everyone to be quiet a moment. He looked at me as if he was looking *through* me, eventually settling his eyes just above my head. "Ladies, this is not just another refugee from one of the other sectors. I think the Father sent Him here for a specific reason."[2]

---

2 See 1 Corinthians 14:24-25.

Derek's keen discernment set me at ease, and I sat back down on the pew. The threesome followed suit. The rays of morning sun moved along the floor as I recounted my story, beginning with the garden and ending with the golden dawn. "There's just one thing I can't figure out. I thought I was having a *spiritual* experience. How am I still here?"

I expected them to be impressed by my story, or at least show some surprise. Instead, they seemed surprised only by my discomfort with what I had experienced.

"Sweetheart, everything you just described is *normal* Christianity now.[3] Through all time, saints have always been appearing before the Father every time they pray. They have always been getting connected stone-on-stone as a spiritual city of Zion.[4] The only thing that's different now is that our eyes have been opened to see all this as plain as day."

Derek waited his turn to explain the new reality, "The spiritual water level has risen now.[5] Evil is much more evident than

---

3 See Colossians 1:27, John 17.
4 See Hebrews 12:22-24.
5 See Ezekiel 47:1-12.

ever before, but so is the Spirit of Holiness. It is not unusual for a visible cloud to show up in our meetings, for angels to greet us at the door, or for saints to travel through the cosmos doing the Father's business. The dead are raised with such frequency that it is not even remarkable anymore. However, we still marvel when someone comes to the Lord.[6] Even translation through space and time is not uncommon anymore because we have begun to lay hold of our eternal inheritance."[7]

As Derek spoke, Lucy was looking at me with the same intensity that Derek had. She waited her turn and added, "You have underestimated the power of consecration. When you give yourself to the Father—heart, mind, spirit, soul, body—He reserves you for Himself.[8] He has the right to take you where He is or send you to any time or place He chooses."

Derek continued his explanation, "The prophetic ministry has come to maturity now, which means that the majority of believers have learned to access heaven directly. In fact,

---

6   See Matthew 10:7-8, Matthew 28:18-20.
7   See Ephesians 2:6, Revelation 4:1, Hebrews 5-8.
8   See Hebrews 12:1-2.

we were just about to go there ourselves to see what the Father would have us pray today."

"You mean, in the Spirit or in the body?" I asked.[9]

"It's the simplest thing you can imagine. We simply consecrate ourselves to Him again and then wait on Him to see what's on His heart. The things we see prophetically in this time are usually confirmed by what we read in the newspaper or internet later.[10] We've seen riots disbanded, storms turned aside, and the dead raised simply because we are praying what the Father shows us."[11]

He still hadn't answered my question, so I reiterated, "But do you ever go in the *body?*"

"What we experience in heaven is actually *more real* than what happens in the body because the Father's eternal realms are where reality is permanently established. However, physical translation usually happens when the Father wants to send us somewhere our body is actually needed—missions trips and

---

9 See 2 Corinthians 12:2.
10 See Deut. 19:15, Matthew 18:16, 2 Cor. 13:1.
11 See John 5:19.

saving people from car wrecks and stuff.[12] It is much more common for the Lord to manifest Himself *here* tangibly. In earlier times, people were surprised if they found a feather or a jewel left behind after they had accessed heaven. Now, God's people have realized that they *are* the Father's jewels.[13] They are beginning to receive spiritual bodies that defy aging, weariness, sickness, and hunger.[14] This is one of the greatest signs that we are encountering a much weightier reality than this present world. As the Father invests His light in us, we are made into children of His light, and the curse of the Fall is removed.[15] This is only part of the inheritance Christ purchased with His blood."

Although I was intrigued by what Derek said, it felt like too much, too soon. I wasn't sure how to take it all in. Just at the point I was beginning to allow disbelief to sneak in, Martha opened her Bible and began reading:

"...you have come to Mount Zion, to the city of the living God, the heavenly

---

[12] See 1 Kings 18:10-12, Acts 8:39.
[13] See Zechariah 9:16, 1 Peter 2:5, Rev. 21:9-14.
[14] See Isaiah 40:31, Rom. 8:11, Philippians 3:20-21.
[15] See Ephesians 5:8-14, 1 Thess. 5:5, 1 John 1:7.

Jerusalem. You have come to thousands upon thousands of angels in joyful assembly, to the church of the firstborn, whose names are written in heaven.

You have come to God, the Judge of all, to the spirits of the righteous made perfect, to Jesus the mediator of a new covenant, and to the sprinkled blood that speaks a better word than the blood of Abel..." (Hebrews 12:22-24)

Martha paused for Derek to explain the passage. It was clear they had worked together like this before, "Notice that it says, 'You *have* come...' This is past tense. Every saint has free access to the Father, the Son, and the Spirit. This doesn't mean praying up, like a telephone line. It means you can encounter the trinity face-to-face with much greater glory than Moses saw."[16]

"The thousands of angels and the cloud of witnesses are just the icing on the cake. We have access to *all of heaven,* which also means *everyone* in heaven. This access has always been available, but until these latter days, very few had the faith or maturity to walk through

---
16 See 2 Corinthians 3:16-18.

the door."[17]

Martha continued reading the chapter, but she did so with words of rebuke in a stern tone, as if she was chastising her granddaughter for stealing a piece of cake:

"See to it that you do not refuse him who speaks. If they did not escape when they refused him who warned them on earth, how much less will we, if we turn away from him who warns us from heaven?

At that time his voice shook the earth, but now he has promised, "Once more I will shake not only the earth but also the heavens." The words "once more" indicate the removing of what can be shaken—that is, created things—so that what cannot be shaken may remain.

Therefore, since we are receiving a kingdom that cannot be shaken, let us be thankful, and so worship God acceptably with reverence and awe, for our "God is a consuming fire." (Hebrews 12:25-28)

Martha had obviously read this passage

---
[17] See Hebrews 10:19-25.

many times and internalized it. She began to preach, *"Do not refuse Him who speaks, for our God is a consuming fire.* But that's just what people have been doing for all the ages. They refuse to hear, and by closing their ears they never get the fire they need to consume 'em and make 'em holy. Really, the only thing that's different now is we have stopped refusing the One Who speaks. And when His fire comes, we step right out of the way and make room for it to burn us right up."[18]

Lucy was beginning to pace the floor, humming. Derek and Martha paused to look at her. Martha broke in, "Well, I think we could all use some refreshments before Lucy gets us started. Let me go fix something."

---

18 See 1 Corinthians 3:10-15.

chapter 5

Going Up

As Lucy tuned her guitar and Martha busied herself in the kitchen, Derek showed me the ropes that rang the old church bell. I gently tugged at the ropes a few times, hearing the bell answer in a clear call that billowed out over the surrounding farms and fields.

Derek opened the front door and let the cool spring air flow in to refresh the old building. We stepped out and stood on the front stoop. The surrounding landscape was vibrant with new spring life—green spikes were bursting through the fertile soil where the neighboring farmer sowed his corn, and cattle grazed in a nearby pasture. Honeybees attended the small orchard on the side of the church, and a few young boys walked together down the road towards the church.

"The honeybees are a miracle." I turned to look back at Derek. "Well, really *all* of this is a miracle."

"When the dust storms came, they carried radioactive poisons, wiping out crops, along with entire populations of songbirds and insects.[1] There's not a thing here that hasn't been prayed back in. Now, our hope is that the refugees we're training to send back out will bring this kind of restoration elsewhere."

The boys waved and walked past the church, continuing their journey towards the old homestead down the road.

"Jim is training those boys in the old ways of planting and harvest, animal husbandry and farming.[2] Later in the month, we will begin teaching them how to pray with power. When they're ready, our community will give them a plot of land of their own to steward.

---

[1] See Deuteronomy 28:15-24.
[2] See Jeremiah 6:16.

Eventually, some may get a call to go back out to the desolate regions."

I remembered the angel's warning when I was taken to see the desolation in China. However, it was tough to even remember that kind of turmoil in this land of refuge.

Derek broke into my thoughts, "Going back out is one of the biggest sacrifices we can make. It's not easy to leave a refuge like this, knowing you'll face persecution, hunger, and hardship."

Martha stood waiting at the door, and handed each of us a glass of sweet tea before we began the next session. "All that being said, boys, it's time to come back in. Lucy is ready."

Derek set up four folding chairs in the open space near the altar, and we sat down in a circle. Derek and Martha said a few prayers, invoking the presence of the Lord and re-consecrating their lives to Him. I closed my eyes and did the same.

Then, Lucy began to sing a spontaneous song of gratitude:

Start the Countdown

"Heavenly father, full of grace
You've hidden us in you
And shown your face
When seas are tossing
We still set sail,
For our anchor holds
Beyond the veil..." [3]

As she sang, a light mist began to fill the room. It carried the same sense of eternal transcendence I had seen in the golden dawn. As I looked into the mist, it quickly brightened. A wind began to blow the mist past me, and with the wind, the room disappeared in a flash of brilliant white light. I felt the thrill of ascension, and just like a cosmonaut on a rocket, my body was glued to the chair from the gravity of what was happening.[4]

To my surprise, I was not alone in this experience. Lucy, Derek, and Martha remained by my side, but they were now joined by countless multitudes who were ascending in the same manner, from different places throughout the region of refuge and around the globe.

---

3 See Hebrews 6:19.
4 See 2 Kings 2:11, *Enoch 39:3*.

Going Up

We passed by fields of stars and the frothing colorful foam of the nebulae, where stars are born. As we passed, I saw beings in the center of them, which were like stars being born, waking up for the first time.[5]

We continued our journey, past oppressive layers of darkness and stretches of chaos that terrified me.[6]

When we came upon the outer reaches, there was an angel with a spear guarding the gate. This guardian was of unimaginable scale, so immense that he dwarfed the milky way. He paid us no attention as we passed through the gate, only to greet an angel that dwarfed the previous one in size and scale. We passed one guardian after another, each one exponentially larger than the previous one. Each had a different weapon. Some were instruments of terrifying punishment. While others were things I had no frame of reference for. The last was a brilliant sword made of lightning.[7]

You would think that this experience

---

5 See Genesis 26:4, Ps. 147:4, Ps. 148:3, Daniel 12:3.
6 See 2 Chronicles 5:13-6:2.
7 See Isaiah 27:1, *Enoch 17:3*.

would make us feel immensely small, but it was just the opposite. With each new angelic encounter, we grew to match the size of the angel we were encountering. By the time we reached the gates of the holy city, everyone was of such an immense size that we regarded each other as equals.[8]

I glanced back at our own planet, tucked away in the folds of space and time. Its weighty and complex problems now seemed simple and miniscule. I knew that we could also *use* the weapons we had seen, if we needed to, for these angels were at the Father's command.

---

8 See 1 John 3:2.

chapter 4

INTO ZION

It became clear to me now that we were moving at the *speed of thought* and that our fuel was *our desire* to meet with the Father. It was a burning love and desire for Him that allowed us to keep pressing deeper and deeper through the cosmos, past the darkness and the waves of radiant light, and into the eternal realms where we belonged.[1]

We approached a wall which was like a translucent plane of crystal, shimmering with colors that went far beyond our earthly spectrum.[2] Our journey ended as we were

---

1 See Song of Solomon 8:6-7.
2 See *Enoch* 14:9-10.

enveloped in lightning and a thunder that shook us to the core. The thunder brought us to the other side. This thunder went beyond what was produced in the earth's atmosphere, for it was not the result of terrestrial weather patterns. Instead of being produced by the updrafts and downdrafts of heat and cold, it was produced by the power of *the Father's eternal light* triumphing over the darkness we were leaving behind in our travels.

As our journey continued, we began moving passed trees whose fruit shown with brilliant light and released an intoxicating fragrance, regenerating us to the core.[3] I wondered what it would be like to taste them, resolving to come back later to linger. I looked up and saw sky again, but much deeper and more beautiful than the sky on earth. It was similar to a turquoise stone, but far deeper in quality.[4] Everything here seemed more dense and substantial than anything on earth. Although the sky had a light of its own, you could still see a tapestry of stars shining in its canopy.

---

3   See *Enoch 24:4-6, Enoch 25:1-7.*
4   See Ezekiel 1:22, Revelation 4:6.

Start the Countdown

A wind began to blow across the landscape, and I heard silver wind chimes begin to release the sound of ringing bells. They were pleasantly musical and perfectly measured, reflecting both the beauty and drama of the moment. Droplets of rain were intermingled in the wind, refreshing us as we flew forward.

The sound of the wind chimes and the now distant eternal thunders were suddenly overshadowed by angelic voices, singing out in abandoned love to the One on the throne. These angels were different than the guardians, for each one's beautiful appearance matched the intricacy of their song. As we approached, an angel turned to look at us with tears running down his face.

He stopped singing for a moment, and I asked him why he was crying.

"What we have waited for is beginning to happen. The Bride is making herself ready.[5] It is even more beautiful than we imagined, and for this we are praising the Father and the Son with a new song."

---
5   See Revelation 19:7.

He started singing, and his voice was louder than anything I had ever heard. Mingled with multitudes of other voices, it sounded like the ebb and flow of ocean tides, only much louder.[6]

As soon as I heard the ebb and flow of worship, my attention was drawn below the golden path we were flying on. A countless multitude of saints was gathered there, each one caught up in his own communion with the Lord.

The light steadily increased as we flew closer to the throne. This light was pure and radiantly white. As it increased, I felt an invigorating energy reaching to the marrow of my bones. It was like bottling up lightning and saving it for later.

Eventually, we came to the *source* of the light, life, and love. The light was so bright that my eyes felt great pain, and I lifted my arm to shield them. To my surprise, this was no comfort at all. The light shone right *through* my forearm, transforming it from a grey, dead thing into a beautiful crystalline

---

6   See Revelation 1:5.

arm through which the light twinkled with beauty. I realized there was no escaping this light, so I put my arm down and yielded myself to it. The light penetrated, removing all that was grey and dead in me and transfiguring my flesh into the glorified body of my inheritance.[7]

I saw a great white throne before me which shone with a terrifying brilliance.[8] I knew the Father and the Son were seated there, but I could not yet make out their features. I could hear the sound of blazing fire and knew this was the sound of the seven Spirits of God blazing around them.[9]

This was when I was first able to hear the Father's voice:

"You have not yet glimpsed the full weight of what my Son accomplished when He shed His blood. Up until now, you have used His sprinkled blood only to lay hold of your own salvation and deliverance. However, this is only the beginning of what He purchased."[10]

7   See 1 Corinthians 15:35-49, Philippians 3:20-21.
8   See Revelation 20:11.
9   See Revelation 4:5.
10 See Colossians 1:15-20.

As He spoke, I saw a single drop of the blood of Christ in my mind's eye.

"Now, I want you to see that there is more light and power in *one drop* of the blood of the Lamb than was released when all the cosmos was created. Now that my Son reigns supremely, the same creative power that was released when I said, "Let there be light!" in the beginning is released every time you apply His blood."[11]

When He said this, the single drop of blood I was beholding now shown with the same brilliant white light streaming from the throne.

"I am raising up a consecrated priesthood who will learn to apply what my Son has already finished. Those who truly believe this will realize they have *already* been given the authority to lift the curse from creation."

As the Father spoke, I felt a combination of love and holy fear. Even though every word shook me to the core, I also felt His great desire

---

11 See John 1.

Start the Countdown

for my intimate friendship on every matter.[12]

---

12 See Exodus 33:11, Job 29:1-6.

chapter 3

THE ROAD HOME

I wanted to linger there a long time. However, the scene quickly faded from me as I began to hear Lucy's voice singing again:

There is no fear in love
For fear has to do with punishment[1]
And You have made us children again
Through the precious blood of the Lamb...

As I opened my eyes, the small church came back into my view. My physical strength returned, and I looked around the room. It was twilight, and the stars were beginning to come out.

---

1 dSee 1 John 4:18.

Derek and Martha opened their eyes too, letting their spiritual senses fade to regain their natural senses.

As beautiful as this experience was, I was left with a lot of questions. I turned to Derek and said, "I have no doubt that what we just encountered was real. However, there is still a sense of division between the *spiritual* and the *natural*."[2]

Derek chuckled and began explaining, "When we encounter the realm of the Spirit, we are walking through the veil that was torn. Simply by going where we went, we have already proven that the separation between heaven and this world has been done away with. However, when we live by the Spirit, then we also *become* the priests—the conduits—for heavenly realities to invade the earth. We should never require signs to demonstrate or prove what we have experienced, because faith is the currency we live by."

---

[2] See 1 Corinthians 2:14, 1 Corinthians 15:46.

Lucy and Martha looked at the floor as he spoke and began excitedly whispering to each other.

I looked down. A field of diamonds lay on the floor beneath us, each sparkling with a light of its own.

Martha broke in, "Well, you talk of not needing signs, but I guess the Lord wants to give 'em anyways."[3]

Lucy grabbed a large bowl from the back of the room, as Martha went down on her hands and knees to begin picking up the diamonds.

"I've seen these kinds of stones before," I said. "I never knew what they were for."

Lucy was carefully picking up each one and examining it before adding it to the bowl. "Some say it means heaven has been accessed here. However, these are much more practical. Diamonds are one of the best barters, and our community has a lot of needs—new livestock, vehicles, more Bibles. This deposit will go a long way."

---

3 See Mark 16:17, Acts 2:43, Acts 5:12.

Derek looked towards the window and then stood up, "Well, I'm nearly starved. How about we go home and get something to eat?"

Lucy excused herself, "My parents probably already have supper on the table, and I need to get going." She poured the bowl of diamonds into a small leather pouch in her backpack. Knowing her family's needs, no one objected. They seemed to already know she was supposed to have them today.[4]

Derek looked back to Martha and me. "Well, I know you all don't have anywhere to go. How about joining me and Rachel for dinner?"

We walked down the road for about two miles, passing abandoned cars and trucks. Farmhouses dotted the landscape, roughly a quarter mile apart. We heard frogs and crickets chatter and croak as we walked along the gravel. Stars began to shine. One could see many more out here in this rural land, away from the hindrance of the mercury lights in the cities.

As we walked, I pondered all I had

---
4 See Acts 4:32.

experienced with this small prayer group today, and what I had seen them declare before. I broke the pleasant silence to press Derek for more insight, "Today, it seemed like much more of a *journey* to enter the presence of God. It also felt more real than anything I have felt before. However, I can't really place my finger on what has changed. I feel refreshed and rejuvenated, but I'm not sure where to go from here."

Martha was the one who answered my question with a clear word of wisdom, "We're just following where Jesus leads the way. Hebrews 4:14 says that we have a great High Priest who has *passed through* the heavens. That's *heavens* plural. In your time, everyone knew that the sprinkled blood of the Lamb bought us eternal life. The only thing different now is that we've learned what we're meant to become *after* we're saved. We are meant to pass through the same heavens He passed through, to commune with the same Father, to administer the same redemption on the basis of the same shed blood. This is what it means to be a priest—to *travel through the heavens* and then release the blessing of heaven on the earth."[5]

As Martha spoke, I could see a distant rocket going up some distance behind her. I wondered to myself if it was the same one the technicians were obsessing about. I wondered how many were being sent.

Derek picked up where she left off, "Jesus Christ is called a 'priest forever in the order of Melchizedek.'[6] He is seated in the eternal realms, which is the place from which He is orchestrating the restoration of all things. However, He has chosen *us* to participate in this restoration, which means we have the authority to release the redemption He already purchased. When we bless someone or the land itself, or even these corn crops we're walking by, we have the power to completely lift off the curse of the Fall and release the kind of perfection that comes from the One on the throne."

Martha interrupted, "Tell him about the corn, too."

---

[5] See Hebrews 5-7.
[6] See Hebrews 5:6.

"Well, we had two years of blight on the corn. Finally, we got the whole community together to pray and bless the fields. We used the same corn seeds this year, but there's no blight here anymore."

I still wasn't satisfied with the answers they gave. "I have heard this theology many times before. However, we never saw the results you are seeing."

"You forgot about the second year. It's not always easy. That was a tough year for us, and we had to keep pressing in until the breakthrough came.[7] There's a *reason* obesity is not a problem anymore."

"We have also realized that it's about much more than the *theology* of the kingdom of heaven. It's about *relationship*. In order to release the light of the face of the Lord to people, or over creation, you first have to spend a lot of time beholding His face. It's like storing up your spiritual battery, so when you need lightning, you already have a store of it in your belly.[8] If our theology doesn't

---

7 See Luke 11:5-13.
8 See John 7:37-39.

lead us to seek His face continually, then it's not really worth much."

As we neared the house, we passed a deer lying on the road. It was mutilated, probably from a rarely seen passing truck, rigged to run on something other than gasoline. Flies were beginning to gather.

Martha stooped down over the deer. She placed her hand on the bloated dead carcass, which caused me to recoil. "Get up now, honey. It's okay. That just wasn't meant to be."

Suddenly, the atmosphere felt electric. My heart began to pound as the deer breathed in a long steady breath and then let out a fierce snort. It thrashed in the gravel for a few seconds, and then stood up and darted away into the brush on the far side of the road.

Even after all I had seen the last few days, this miracle left me at a loss for words.

Martha turned to explain, "At the end of the day, it's about loving like the Father loves. He doesn't just love you and me. He loves all of creation 'cause He made it. And Jesus didn't just die for you and me. He died so *all* creation would be restored."

I knew it would be foolish to ask *how*. Things were becoming clearer now. Seek the face of the Lord. Bask in His light and love. Then, you'll have enough of it to restore everything else around you.

As we approached the small farm house, Rachel opened a creaky screen door to greet us cheerfully. After Derek introduced me, Rachel invited us to the table, gesturing to the chairs.

chapter 2

SETTING THE TABLE

I'll let you all get acquainted," Derek said, as he pulled out a chair for Rachel and began setting the table. A crock pot of beef stew was simmering on the serving stand in the dining room, and the scent of fresh, hot biscuits wafted in from the kitchen. Derek began to slice fresh tomatoes and cucumbers from their small greenhouse as I told my story to Rachel, who was now bouncing their young toddler, Aaron, on her knee. The tousle-haired boy bore a keen resemblance to his father. He was thumbing through magazines several decades old.

Now it was Rachel's turn to tell her stories. Derek brought in a basket of hot biscuits, cold mint tea, and a simple Israeli salad of diced tomatoes and cucumbers. As we ate, Rachel began telling me about her life before she came to this region of refuge.

"In those days, no one really knew or cared what was going on outside their own little world. We were all constantly looking at our screens—television screens, computer screens, screens on phones and watches. Even screens on appliances and dashboards and dining tables in restaurants. They even did away with cashiers at the grocers and the chain stores, replacing them with *more* screens.

It got to where people hardly knew how to talk to each other anymore. I didn't realize until later how *impersonal* we all were, even with our own family and friends. It was all about *looking* a certain way, trying not to offend people, creating the illusion of happiness, but in reality, we were all very alone."

"That sounds a lot like 2016." I said with a knowing smile.

"Yes, but it got much worse. As more and more robots and computers replaced our jobs, mankind began to lose our purpose entirely. We were lost in a sea of our own comfort and technology, disconnected from each other and from the Lord. We had everything we could want, but nothing we really *needed*."

"Strangely, the attacks on the infrastructure were one of the biggest blessings we could have had. If that system had not collapsed, I don't think we ever would have resolved to build a better one. It's not that we didn't see the benefits of new technology. It's that we lost our connection to the old ways, the ancient paths. We forgot the lessons passed down to us and had to re-learn them the hard way."

Rachel winked at Derek, and he began clearing plates. "You know, it's like what Derek's doing now. When we clear off the table, it just makes room for the next course. Hard times are kind of like clearing the table, removing all the old or bad ways of doing things to make room for something much better."[1]

---

1 See Haggai 2:6-9.

Derek returned with a still-warm blackberry pie, followed by tall glasses of milk. After spending years drinking skim milk, it took some adjustment to enjoy milk so fresh and thick with cream.

I began to wonder more about the state of the world in these times and spurted out a steady stream of questions: "How many regions of refuge are there? How far does the desolation stretch? What is going on with the governments in the world?"

They looked at each other for a moment, and then Derek spoke with clarity, "People used to think they had every event of the end times figured out. But it's just this simple: The dark gets a lot darker, and the light gets a lot brighter.[2] Many governments have already collapsed under the strain of environmental turmoil, war, and economic upheaval. Many nations have oscillated between anarchy and tyranny. Even our own government went through this process, as my marks bear." Derek rolled up his sleeve to show a tattoo on His forearm, signifying a darker time in his life.

---

2 See Isaiah 60:1-3.

"Where'd you get that?" I asked, feeling a deep foreboding as I looked at the strange shapes on his arm, trying to make sense of them. He looked at Aaron for a moment, studying the little boy's innocence. He turned back to me and answered, "A good question, for another time."

Derek promptly rolled his sleeve back down and took a long drink of cold, fresh milk. I have learned not to pry veterans to tell their stories when they are not ready to share them.

He continued, "Despite these perils, the kingdom of God is now advancing much more than ever before. The spiritual water levels have risen in these times, and we are getting reports all the time about whole towns, villages, and even regions being saved. Remember, the Bible promises that there will be 'a great multitude' beyond what anyone in heaven or earth can count."[3]

Martha gave Derek a grave look and then turned to me, "We also face daily battles because there has been an awakening. It's

---

3 See Revelation 7:9.

a lot like when Elijah was confronting the prophets of Baal on Mt. Carmel.[4] There are regions covered with drought and blight, despair and depression, because the powers of darkness have taken root in wicked hearts and corrupt governments. There is idolatry beyond what you would believe if I told you, and along with that, great cruelty and suffering. Many of our missionaries to other regions have already been martyred in horrific ways. We've also had plenty of terrorism and violence, trying to get inroads in this region.[5] About fifty people lost their lives in a bombing at a church just south of here a few months ago. Funny thing is, many of them saw prophetically that it would happen and went to church anyways. That's when my husband Jimmy went to be with the Lord."

As Martha spoke, Aaron dropped his magazines and began pointing. "Look, mommy. Angels!"

---

[4] See 1 Kings 18:16-46.
[5] See Matthew 11:12.

The Road Home

As soon as he said this, we all could see them too. The angels stood surrounding the table, pure and resolute.

The one nearest to the door was familiar to me, but now seemed taller and wore far more glorious clothing than when we first met. He turned to me and stretched out his hand. "It's time. You have what you need now."

For some reason, I looked back at the magazines, wishing I could bring them with me to see what would happen between my own time and this one. The angel smiled and reassured me, "You already have all you need."

As I took his outstretched hand, a portal opened around us, and the dining room vanished. I realized too late that I forgot to say "goodbye."

chapter 1

THE LAUNCH PAD

The angel let go of my hand once my feet were standing on solid ground again. As the portal closed, he vanished with it. I was deposited back into my garden. The sun was in the same spot in the sky. The rabbit at the back of the garden was still munching on the same bunch of lettuce. The fragrance of rosemary and mint filled the atmosphere again as I walked to the sundial. Its shadow was just where it had been when I left.

I laughed heartily and walked up the stairs to my house, bringing with me the basket of fresh produce and eggs that I set out to collect in the first place. "Probably a good time to start journaling," I said aloud to myself.[1]

I filled the crock pot with everything we would need for chicken-lime soup and got my sons ready to leave for our afternoon prayer and worship session at the Bob Jones Vision Center (BJVC).

As we drove on I-485, I shared with them the parts of my prophetic experience that I felt they could handle at their young ages. Raising children isn't just about keeping them *happy*, but also keeping their imagination healthy and alive.[2]

The meeting was already underway at the BJVC as we arrived. My wife Rachelle would join us in the early evening after a much needed coffee date with her friends. I gave the boys a canvas bag full of legos and some banners, and sat down to listen to what the people were hearing from the Lord today.

Robert began sharing his heart, but he was more preaching than praying,

---

1 See Habakkuk 2:2-3.
2 See Matthew 18:3, Matthew 19:14.

"The landing pad for the great glory that we will encounter in the future is our *faithfulness* and *desire* for the Lord in the here and now. The place where His glory will rest in the greatest magnitude is in the hearts and minds of saints who continue their pursuit even on mundane, boring days.[3]

"You want to move from glory to glory in the future? Then begin moving in greater longing and desire for God now.[4] Begin building the relationships that will sustain you on the journey. Begin to trace the lines of the prophetic history that's been handed to you and see how you fit in the long trajectory of what the Father is doing. For you have a legacy of many generations before you, and the things that happen in this place will impact many generations that follow you."

As he continued to preach, Rachelle sat down next to me and greeted me with a kiss. I placed my arm around her, and we listened together.

The prophetic music night team began to

---

[3] See Galatians 6:9.
[4] See Psalm 63, 2 Corinthians 3:16-18.

tune up, and other people began arriving as Robert continued to preach.

"One of the prophesies we are all a part of is, we are called to raise up a *city of refuge*. However, it is actually much more than this. When the Moravians planted houses of prayer throughout this region, they established a vast *region of refuge* which stretches through South Carolina, North Carolina, and Tennessee. This region extends far to the north, through Virginia, Maryland, Pennsylvania, New York, all the way up to Ontario. This region will be a place where the lampstands burn so brightly for generations to come that no darkness will be able to snuff them out.[5]

"In the hour when turmoil and darkness flood the East Coast and the Mississippi River Valley, the West Coast and the four corners area, this region will provide a refuge for many and send out aid workers and missionaries to bring in an unfathomable harvest.

"How do we raise up this region of refuge? How do we build the landing pad for the greater glory to rest? We must be faithful to

---

5 See Matthew 5:13-16.

walk out the prophetic instructions we have already received. Bob Jones prophesied that this place would be like 'the greatest show on earth.' He said it would be a 'three-ring circus,' fusing 'prayer, praise, and prophesy.'

"However, there is even more than what he saw. For the tent that overshadows this 'circus' is a canopy of angelic protection that will stretch over this entire region. The tent stakes are the places where other fellowships are raised up—some for prophetic intercession and others for evangelism and discipleship. We have a role in raising up and supporting *all* these expressions of the kingdom."

A line of people began to form. Everyone who had a burden to pray or prophesy began to pray *regional* prayers, to call forth a canopy of protection over this vast region of refuge.

As the prophetic music night band began to play, Rachelle left my side and began dancing with banners, the billowing white silk symbolizing the angelic canopy descending on the region as we prayed. A young boy named Derek, about seven years old who was visiting Morningstar with his family from rural Pennsylvania, grabbed the microphone and began to declare with power,

"And it shall come to pass that he who is left in Zion and remains in Jerusalem will be called holy—everyone who is recorded among the living in Jerusalem.

"When the Lord has washed away the filth of the daughters of Zion, and purged the blood of Jerusalem from her midst, by the spirit of judgment and by the spirit of burning, then the Lord will create above every dwelling place of Mount Zion, and above her assemblies, a cloud and smoke by day and the shining of a flaming fire by night.

<u>For over all the glory there will be a</u> covering. And there will be a tabernacle for shade in the daytime from the heat, for a place of refuge, and for a shelter <u>from storm</u> and rain" (Isaiah 4:3-6).

As the young boy spoke, I realized there was something familiar about his face, his voice. I was trying to place where we may have met before, when I suddenly felt a familiar sensation. As all those present at the meeting came before the Father in prayer, it felt as though the whole room was literally ascending with us.

As we ascended together, I realized this was only the beginning of a long trajectory of restoration that will last many decades. However, seeing the end goal, I was deeply satisfied to realize I was not alone in this adventure into uncharted waters.

I considered all the promises I had seen, all the warnings, and then looked again at this small group, many of whom were now overcome in ecstasies of revelation or travailing with deep moans as the heart and mind of the Father was revealed to them. I realized this house of prayer was our ship. This small group of friends was really a noble band of trustworthy comrades on an upward journey through the decades of restoration to come and on into the eternal shores in the distance. I leaned back in my chair, smiling under the weight of God's peace, and said, *"Make it so, Lord. Make it so."*

Afterword

This book explores what it may look like for a small community when they discover the power and authority available to every believer through what Christ has accomplished. I hope this writing highlights **"Christ and Him crucified"** as the most important message for us to cling to in troubled times (see 1 Corinthians 2:2).

In the western world, we have long held an evangelical religious heritage that values *salvation,* but neglects the deeper and more transformative aspects of our faith in Christ. As we move forward into the next move of God, the Lord is going to restore truths and mysteries of the Spirit that go far beyond anything seen before. However, the towering heights of spiritual insight, wisdom, and understanding soon to rise will rest upon the strong foundation of simple faith in Christ we have inherited from the generations preceding us.

BUILDING "REGIONS OF REFUGE"

The central premise of this book is, the Father is going to raise up "regions of refuge" for His people in the last days. These will be places where worship, intercession, evangelism, and discipleship have been so effective that great restoration begins to take place in people and in creation itself.

The most obvious biblical support for this concept is drawn from the Old Testament's depiction of "cities of refuge" (see Numbers 35:6-34). These were cities for those who were rightly convicted of crimes to flee to for safety from avengers. They were places where *mercy* is clearly demonstrated.

These cities were sovereignly identified by God. People would not have known where

Afterword

to flee in their hour of judgment, unless God marked these cities first, telling them which ones were destined to be safe havens.

Likewise, the first key to identifying the destiny of different regions is to ask the Father what *He* is saying about them. A good follow-up question to this is, "Father, where do you want *me* to be planted?" While we have an important role in bringing righteousness to these regions by administrating what Christ has done, these are ultimate *sovereign expressions* of God's mercy for us.

At first glance, applying the promise of "cities of refuge" to ourselves seems at odds with New Testament teaching. For example, when discussing martyrdom, Jesus made it clear that **"no servant is greater than his master. If they persecuted me, they will persecute you also" (John 15:20).**

Likewise, Daniel made it clear that there will be a point in history when the antichrist arises to **"destroy those who are mighty, the holy people,"** and they will be **"delivered into his hands"** for a limited period of time (see Daniel 7:25, 8:24). I am well aware of these perilous predictions in scripture. Some have lived in dread of these things being fulfilled.

However, we have ignored the other side of the coin for too long. In the same chapter, we also read, **"the Ancient of Days came and pronounced judgment in favor of the holy people of the Most High, and the time came when they possessed the kingdom" (Daniel 7:22).**

Most Christian literature about the end times has highlighted the role of the anti-Christ, while neglecting the predicted rise of God's holy ones. My goal of this book is to provide insight into what it will look like when we truly become the holy and spiritual people we are predicted to become in Christ.

The deeper biblical support for raising up "regions of refuge" is simply an expansion of the truths in Genesis 28. As in Jacob's dream, the "house of God" is meant to be a place where the literal and tangible presence of God comes to rest. In Jacob's dream, the house of God is a place where a "gateway to heaven" is established through which the angels of

Afterword

God ascend and descend to bring restoration to the earth and to the heart of mankind. The portrayal of the three intercessors in Pennsylvania was meant to illustrate the reality of this promise, as well as the central importance of houses of prayer in raising up and maintaining regions of refuge in the future.

The true house of God is not found in isolated individuals or mere church buildings. The place where the Father will choose to take up *permanent residence* is in the New Jerusalem, a spiritual city populated by countless living saints, the cloud of witnesses, and multitudes of angels. This city, which Paul tells us we have *already* come to, embodies the full promise of restoration that Christ purchased.[1]

In this city, **"there is no more death, mourning, crying, or pain, for the old order of things has passed away" (Revelation 21:4)**. In this city, there are streams of living water continually flowing down golden streets. In this city, there is a completely restored heaven and earth, and

---

1 See Hebrews 12:22-24.

Start the Countdown

the curse of the Fall is removed entirely.

The heart of man and creation itself are crying out for this greater reality to be fully unveiled. However, since we have *already* come to this city by the Spirit, we already have access to whatever level of restoration we have the faith to lay hold of. Prayer, worship, and prophecy are the means by which we access this restoration for ourselves and release it to all those people and places in our sphere of influence. This is the basic purpose of priestly ministry under the new covenant, which all believers are called to be a part of.[2]

As we begin to access rising levels of restoration today, entire regions will be set aside for God's glory to be revealed. This great restoration begins as a small seed hidden in our hearts. However, as in the parable of the mustard seed, this small seed will continue growing and expanding until it has the power to transform and preserve creation itself.

This may even be what Jesus was hinting at when he said that this kingdom tree, when

---

2 See 1 Peter 2:9.

Afterword

fully grown, would become a refuge so great that **"the birds of the air come and nest in its branches" (Matthew 13:32).** When the kingdom of God is fully revealed, it provides a refuge and over-shadowing glory to all who enter it.

The reason I am confident we can experience this kind of restoration in this life is because I place all of my confidence and hope in what the scriptures declare about Christ's supremacy. Paul wrote:

"The Son is the image of the invisible God, the firstborn over all creation. For in him all things were created: things in heaven and on earth, visible and invisible, whether thrones or powers or rulers or authorities; all things have been created through him and for him.

He is before all things, and in him all things hold together. And he is the head of the body, the church; he is the beginning and the firstborn from among the dead, so that in everything he might have the supremacy. For God was pleased to have all his fullness dwell in him, and through him to reconcile to himself all things, whether things on earth or things in heaven,

by making peace through his blood, shed on the cross"**(Colossians 1:15-20).**

As the Creator of the universe, Christ was already supreme before He went to the cross. He was already holding the universe together by the **"word of his power" (Hebrews 1:3)**. The promise we inherit from our evangelical heritage is that Jesus gave Himself as a sacrifice to remove the burden of sin and the curse of the Fall. For this reason, we already recognize that sin, darkness, and our carnal nature can be completely removed from our lives. Likewise, the promise of the "regions of refuge" is based on the premise that Christ's sacrifice entails levels of power and authority we have not yet explored.

We have not yet done the **"greater works" (John 14:12)** that Jesus said we would do. We have not yet spoken to a mountain to move, rearranging the geography around us (Matthew 17:20). However, the times are coming when we will have a full revelation of the overwhelming authority Christ purchased for us when He died. For He did not die only to give us free "fire insurance," He died to **"reconcile to himself all**

Afterword

things" (Colossians 1:20). He died to bring a full restoration of greater glory to the entire cosmos.

Having purchased this authority to restore all things, He has now handed the keys to us. Now we are called to overcome by carrying the full authority and restorative power that Christ granted us as His priests. The scriptures tell us we are becoming **"a kingdom and priests to serve our God and [we] will reign on the earth" (see Revelation 5:10).** We have crossed the threshold of salvation, but have yet to explore the full weight of restorative power the Father wants to release through us as **"priests forever in the order of Melchizedek" (Hebrews 7:17).**

There is no losing scenario for believers. Whether in this life or the next, we will all inherit the glory and complete restoration that we hope for. Even if we are called to be martyrs, we inherit a great glory as soon as our last breath is exhaled, far exceeding and compensating us for any trial we may have faced in this life. Persecution also brings out the very best in us individually and as a body, because it purges weakness, complacency, and godlessness from our lives.

From a much simpler point of view, the "region of refuge" described in this book is simply an illustration of what happens when we become the kind of "salt and light" that Jesus Christ said we would be (Matthew 5:13-15). If we lose our saltiness and hide our light as He warned, then we will certainly inherit a darker and more corrupt future as a nation.

However, I trust that much greater things are in store for us. I hold on to the promise that the Father is raising up a glorious Bride who will become everything the Lord dreamed she would be when He gave His life to purchase her.

I wanted to include a map of the region of refuge I have seen. However, now is not the time, for its borders are not yet established, and its shining towers have yet to be raised. Instead, I present this story to plant the *seed of possibility* in the hearts of those who read it. Our mandate to restore creation springs from our mandate to restore man because all of creation was placed under man's dominion

Afterword

in the beginning.[3] We have the authority to release redemption *on the land* because we have the authority to release redemption *in the heart of mankind.* And which is greater, the creation or the beings to which our God subjected creation's fate?

RE-EXAMINING OUR ESCHATOLOGY

When Jesus Christ was incarnated in human flesh through the power of the Spirit, there were very few that recognized Him. The fulfillment of every ancient prophecy came in a manner that the leading religious scholars of that time could not recognize. While they were looking in a palace, Jesus was born in a run-down stable. While they were looking for a warrior-king like David to deliver them, Jesus came to serve others with compassion and die for our sins. The warrior-king they hoped for is still coming, but their interpretation of prophecy missed the mark.

While some rejected Christ because they did not accept His ways, most of the scholars of Jesus' day did not recognize Him because

---

3 See Genesis 1:26-28.

they used logical reasoning and speculation about the ancient prophecies handed to them. Instead of searching out ancient prophecies with the assistance of the same Holy Spirit and the same angelic ministry that accompanied it in the beginning, they tried to interpret deep and mystical truths through mere human reasoning. This is a well-traveled road to miss what God is doing.

The ones who recognized Christ were those who followed Him and began building the city He envisioned. They were people who allowed the Spirit of the Lord to guide their steps, as they learned to balance their knowledge of the scriptures with a keen sense of renewed spiritual life. They learned to grow in character by the Spirit's inner working, moved in power and spiritual gifts, and worked regularly with angels in their midst.

Likewise, there are many different interpretations about how the last days of earth's history will unfold. Most of these are wrong because we have often drawn conclusions about what the ancient prophecies of the Bible mean, using little

Afterword

more than human speculation, logic, and religious tradition.

No one can have a clear interpretation of what will unfold before the day of Christ's return apart from what the scriptures and the Holy Spirit reveal. Some have seen prophetic glimpses of certain events, and there are some eschatological positions based on the Bible that I agree with. However, the wisest path we can take is to become reacquainted with the living Christ and fall in love with Him again.

It is our relationship with the Spirit of Christ that will sustain us in troubled times, give us the hope to keep persevering, and plant in our hearts the faith to change the atmosphere and landscape around us. My concern is that all of the chatter about ancient nephilim resurfacing, antichrists arising, and governments persecuting us have created a bunker mentality, leading us astray from our first love and our greater purpose.

Instead of building the glorious city the Lord has dreamed about, we have set our eyes and our attention on the Babylon that surrounds us. Let us now shift our focus back to what the Father is doing, for the best way to combat the rising tide of darkness in the earth is to begin building the city, and nurturing the Bride, who will stand to vanquish it once and for all.

ABOUT THE STORY

This story begins and ends at real places. I really do have a lovely garden with a sundial and paths lined with rosemary and mint. I often do linger there and watch the rabbits at the back of the garden eat my lettuce (I have enough of it to share with them). Likewise, the Bob Jones Vision Center is currently in the final stages of its construction. Robert in the story is my friend Robert Rummage, our intercession pastor at Morningstar Fellowship.

Although his words in the story are mine, I wanted to demonstrate that we will each play different roles as the next move of God unfolds. Even the small church in rural Pennsylvania is a real place. The one who actually let me ring the bell so that it echoed out over the surrounding pastures was Harlan

Afterword

Holland, my beloved grandfather.

The real places in this story are like bookends that ground the revelations shared in between. However, I do not consider these revelations to be any *less real* than the garden I weed every week.

The first angel in the dream appeared to me in a vivid dream about two years ago, showing me many of the revelations in this book in the watches of the night. I had to research my family tree to verify some of the things I was told about my ancestor Harry Ritter.

I believe the region of refuge I was shown by the Lord is one of many that He will raise up. The center of the region I was shown runs along the historic Great Philadelphia Wagon Road, a road that runs from Pennsylvania to South Carolina. This road runs through the previous expansive territory of the former Heritage USA grounds and even through Billy Graham's grandparents' backyard. Most of Route 81 was built on this historic wagon road. This wagon road is the central road through which these rural regions were settled and was often frequented by Moravian missionaries who planted houses of prayer along the way.

On August 14 of 2014 (8/14), I also had a dream about this region of refuge, and this trail of revival legacy, running northwards through what I refer to as the "814 corridor"—the telephone area code for a large swath of central Pennsylvania. I believe this region of refuge has specific bright places, where great lampstands will be raised up, such as in Rochester and Buffalo, New York, and Toronto and Hamilton, Ontario, at its northern reaches. The area of these four cities is called the "golden horseshoe." Years ago, Bob Jones prophesied that this would be the region where the "hoof of the white warhorse of the Lord" would be firmly planted to release revival to the surrounding region. This is also the region where the second great awakening began under the leadership of Charles Finney.

I suspect there are many other "regions of refuge" the Lord desires to raise up. I have been shown this particular region because I have deep roots in it and a burden to pray for

Afterword

it. Now, you must ask the Lord what region you should be praying in to. There may be another region of refuge that only you can begin to envision and map out.

I agree with Terry Bennett's eschatology on these matters. Although he has released stern prophetic warnings about the shaking that is coming in the end times, he has also prophesied that there will be some "sheep nations" and regions where the kingdom is established in such power that the antichrist cannot fully dominate there. As I will present in my forthcoming book, *The Rise of His Holy Ones*, we must begin to see the end times as a two-sided coin. One side of the coin is marked, "rising glory and harvest" and the other side is marked, "judgement and shaking." We must keep both aspects of what is coming on our radar in order to be fully prepared for the future.

I have boldly shared this story because the Father wants *every believer* to **"follow the way of love and eagerly desire the gifts of the Spirit, especially prophecy"** (1 Corinthians 14:1). The kinds of revelation I record in this book are a conglomeration of real spiritual experiences. However, these experiences are available to *everyone* who eagerly desires them, for we live in the hour when the Spirit is being poured out on **"all flesh"** so that **"everyone will prophesy" (Joel 2:28)**.

The Father loves each one of us dearly and eagerly desires *our* company much more than we could ever desire *His* company. We serve the same God who desperately cried out, **"Where are you?"** when Adam and Eve first sinned in the garden (Genesis 3:9). Accustomed to His daily time with them, He was grieved when they failed to show up in His presence on that day. The great waves of restoration and glory that we will see in the future begin with the smallest and most humble acts imaginable—a few prayers uttered in our morning commute, an open Bible with a morning cup of coffee, a choice to speak well of everyone around us, even when we are hurt. We have access to limitless love, light, glory, and power. However, God has chosen to reveal these things in the humble circumstances of our lives, just as Christ was born in a stable. Paul explained,

"For God, who said, "Let light shine out of darkness," made his light shine in our hearts to give us the light of the knowledge of God's

Afterword

glory displayed in the face of Christ.

"But we have this treasure in jars of clay to show that this all-surpassing power is from God and not from us. We are hard pressed on every side, but not crushed; perplexed, but not in despair; persecuted, but not abandoned; struck down, but not destroyed.

"We always carry around in our body the death of Jesus, so that the life of Jesus may also be revealed in our body" (2 Corinthians 4:6-10).

Just like jars of clay, we can sense the frailty and brokenness of our own lives. We are well aware of our daily trials and challenges. However, if we set our affections on the "light of the knowledge of the glory of God" that resides in Christ's face, then we will learn to transcend and overcome every challenge we encounter, beginning in our own hearts and minds. The restoration of entire regions throughout the earth and the restoration of whole nations begin with broken people who choose to *set their affections* on the Lord of Glory *right now*.

OTHER BOOKS BY MICHAEL FICKESS
Available from Morningstar Publications.

ENOCH'S BLESSING:
A Modern Paraphrase of Enoch's Ancient Writings

PATHS OF EVER-INCREASING GLORY
What Enoch's Ancient Writings Reveal about Christ's Supremacy and Our Prophetic Destiny

THE RESTORATION OF ALL THINGS
A Prophetic Allegory

Visit **www.michaelfickess.com**
for free podcasts, timely prophetic insights, devotional readings, new releases, and more!

Thank you for supporting Michael's ministry with your purchase and with your prayers.

Made in the USA
Charleston, SC
19 August 2016